The World of Mosses

The World of
MOSSES

written and illustrated by Bette J. Davis

Lothrop, Lee & Shepard Company. New York

Lothrop Books by Bette J. Davis

The World of Mosses
Winter Buds
Freedom Eagle
Musical Insects
Mole From the Meadow

For Roni

My thanks to Dr. Thomas Lee,
of St. Anselm's College, for checking
this book for botanical accuracy.

H.96

Library of Congress Cataloging in Publication Data

Davis, Bette J.
  The world of mosses.

    SUMMARY:A study of the life cycle, growth patterns, and importance of mosses.
    1. Mosses—Juvenile literature.   [1. Mosses]   I. Title.
QK537.5.D38   588′.2   74-10606
ISBN 0-688-41667-5
ISBN 0-688-51667-X   (lib. bdg.)

Contents

·1·

Bits of Beauty

Forests of elfin trees, tufts of tiny leaves, wisps of color-ful fruit: all form the miniature world of mosses. Explore the woods during spring and summer and you will discover these delicate plants. A single step can take you from a slick floor of brown pine needles onto a luxuriant carpetlike expanse of green mosses. Look around and notice the brilliance of green rosettes at-tached to decaying logs and wet rocks. Stroll down the shady side of a ravine or walk by a waterfall and you will find plush cushions of moss. Look into and near streams and ponds or in places that are sometimes sub-merged in water.

Mosses are particularly abundant in cool, moist woods where old stumps are rotting. But many of them grow in dry, open places, such as fields and roadsides.

City dwellers can find moss in vacant lots and in parks. Sometimes it creeps through the cracks of sidewalks. If you search, you can find mosses growing in all sorts of places. With the help of a guidebook, you can identify many of these tiny, delicate plants. Each species of moss has its own characteristics as well as an individual growth pattern.

Examine moss under a magnifying glass, and you will see that it is far more complex than it appears to the naked eye. What looks like soft green wool is actually a mass of tiny plants. Some mosses stand erect. They resemble miniature trees with straight trunks and delicately formed leaves that grow from the base to the tip. Other mosses trail over the ground like tiny velvety vines. Like a tangled web, they interlace with one another to form a thick, dense mat. Still others look like tiny feathery ferns.

Wherever moss grows, it adds a bit of color. You will be attracted by the rich dark green clumps, or the lush emerald green carpets of moss. But although moss is always some shade of green, it is occasionally accented by touches of red, orange, or yellow. This is the fruit of the moss plant, often as small as a flower seed sitting atop a threadlike stem.

Throughout winter, moss lies cold and asleep like lilliputian evergreens awaiting the warmth of spring to grow again. It then reproduces—rapidly spreading its blanket of green over much of the earth.

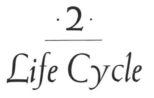

·2·
Life Cycle

Scientists have divided the vast kingdom of plants into numerous divisions called *phyla*. Of the four main divisions, the first and simplest phylum consists of algae, fungi, and lichens. The second division, or phylum, is called *Bryophyta*. Mosses, which scientists call *Musci,* and liverworts, which scientists call *Hepaticae,* are the two classes that make up this second phylum of the plant world. The third phylum, more complex than the Bryophytes, includes ferns, horsetails, and ground pines. The fourth and most complicated division contains the flowering or seed plants. This group contains more members than all the other groups put together and has the greatest variety of form and habit. It ranges from duckweed, no bigger than the head of a pine, to the giant sequoia, the tallest of all trees.

Of all plants, the one-celled algae (members of the simplest phylum) are best suited for aquatic life. The third phylum (ferns and their relatives) and the fourth phylum (seed-producing plants) survive best on land. But Bryophyta, the phylum to which mosses belong, can live both on land and water like the amphibious frogs and turtles of the animal kingdom. For this reason, Bryophytes are often referred to as the amphibians of the plant world.

All Bryophytes are independent plants because they contain chlorophyll. They are able to make their own food. Chlorophyll is the green coloring found in leaves and other parts of plants. It enables the living tissue of plants, the protoplasm, to absorb energy from sunlight and convert "dead" or inorganic chemicals into "life-giving" or organic chemicals. This is the process known as *photosynthesis*.

Most people think of a green plant as one that grows from a seed and eventually produces more seeds from which new plants grow. But mosses are green plants that grow from *spores* instead of seeds. Spores resemble seeds somewhat, but they are much tinier. Invisible, except under a microscope, these unicellular bodies are produced in such tremendous quantities that they float in the air all around us. A mass of spores can look like a small puff of dust. Like a seed, a spore develops into an infant plant.

The process by which most moss plants reproduce is

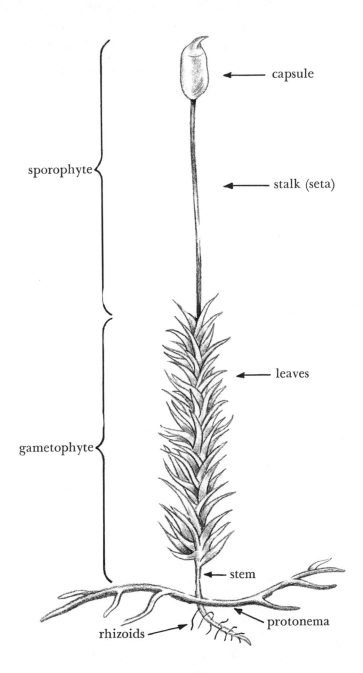

capsule

stalk (seta)

sporophyte

leaves

gametophyte

stem

protonema

rhizoids

Moss Plant

very curious. The life cycle consists of two distinct phases, sexual and asexual. The sexual phase produces eggs and *sperms,* called *gametes.* The asexual phase produces spores. Each phase produces the other, and this process is referred to as the alternation of generations. These two generations are called *gametophyte* and *sporophyte,* that is, gamete plant and spore plant.

The sexual phase of the plant begins its growth from an asexual spore. The spore produces a tiny, threadlike, and trailing structure called a *protonema.* The protonema branches and spreads over the ground. Minute buds form on the branches and develop into the leafy plants that most people recognize as moss. At the tips of the leafy shoots, entirely hidden by the leaves, are many reproductive or sex organs. They are microscopic, but the male buds can often be detected by the rosette of bractlike leaves (petals) that surround them and are often green, red, or orange.

Some species bear both male and female organs on the same plant. Other species have the male organs on one plant and the female organs on another. Inside the male organs, called *antheridia,* are little free-swimming sperm. These are the male sex cells called *antheridium.* The antheridia bursts open and releases the sperms or antheridium. With a light coating of dew or other moisture on the leaves, the sperm swims by means of hairlike appendages called *cilia,* over to the female sex organs called *archegonia.* Inside each female organ is a single egg, the female sex cell called *arche-gonium*. One sperm enters the female organ and unites with the single egg. The union of sperm and egg is called fertilization and results in the formation of a fertilized egg called a *zygote*.

Fertilization starts the second or asexual phase of the cycle. The zygote remains in the female organ. It immediately begins to grow and produces the sporophyte, a plant quite different in structure and appearance from the male and female plants. A long hairlike stalk grows up and out of the leafy shoot of the plant. The top of the stalk swells and becomes a capsule, also known as the "fruit." Inside the capsule are many spores. These are also reproductive cells, but they are neither male nor female. Since the spores in the spore case multiply entirely by cell division, and not by the union of egg and sperm, they are asexual. The stalk and the capsule both contain chlorophyll and carry on photosynthesis, but most of their nourishment comes from the parent plant. The sporophyte soaks up its nourishment by a little absorbent lump embedded in the leaves of the parent plant at the base of the stalk.

When the spores are ripe, the spore case opens and releases them. The winds scatter them far and wide. If they fall where conditions are favorable, they grow into a new protonema which is the beginning of the sexual phase. The old cycle is complete and a new cycle begins. The moss plant that we see in the forest or on a

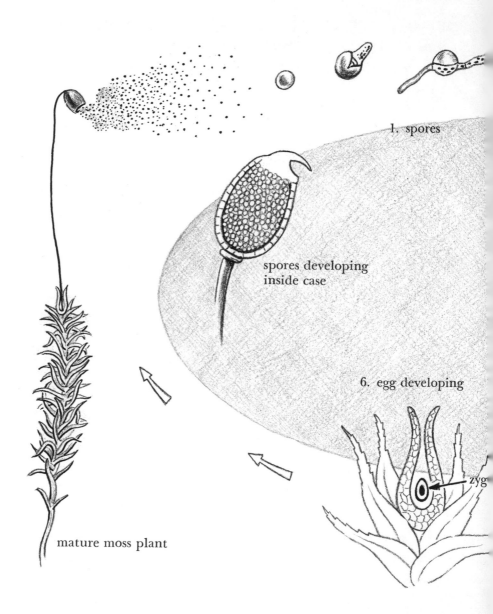

1. spores

spores developing
inside case

6. egg developing

zyg

mature moss plant

Life Cycle

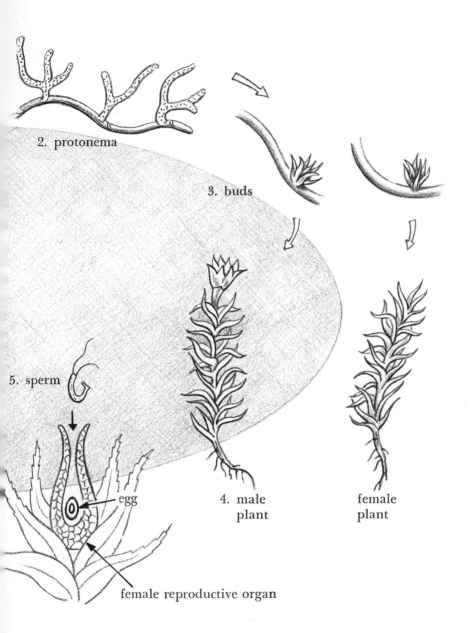

2. protonema

3. buds

5. sperm

egg

female reproductive organ

4. male
plant

female
plant

roadside is only one small aspect of the life cycle.

The sporophytes of mosses have many interesting parts. The thin, frail stalk on which the capsule, or fruit, is borne is called a *seta*. Setae vary in length on different plants. When the stalk is very short, the fruit is almost hidden from view in the surrounding leaves. Some setae stretch high above the moss plants, clearly displaying their tiny fruit.

Capsules have many special features that protect the spores until they are mature. On top is a hoodlike structure, covering the young capsule, called a *calyp-tra*. It usually falls off before the spores are ripe. But if it remains until the capsule fills out, it is often pushed upwards until it covers only the beak of the

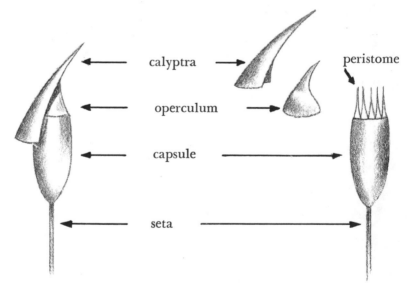

calyptra

operculum

capsule

peristome

seta

Capsule

hood-shaped   like a beaked cap

Shapes of the Calyptra

convex   cone-shaped   short-beaked   long-beaked

Shapes of the Operculum

capsule lid. In a few mosses, the calyptra is covered with hairs.

Nearly all of the moss capsules open by means of a lid, or *operculum,* located under the calyptra. This tiny lid can be curved, cone-shaped, short-beaked, or long-beaked. Underneath the lid, surrounding the mouth of the capsule, is a tiny single or double fringe called the *peristome.* The outer fringe is composed of strands or "teeth" that are extremely sensitive to moisture. The color of these strands usually varies from shades of red to orange to yellow.

The inner peristome, more delicate than the outer, is divided into segments. In wet weather the teeth close tightly together to prevent the ripened spores from washing away. When they are dry, they separate and bend backward, allowing the spores to sift out slowly and scatter. The size, shape, and number of teeth are often important in determining the species of a particular moss plant. By using a microscope you can see the peristome.

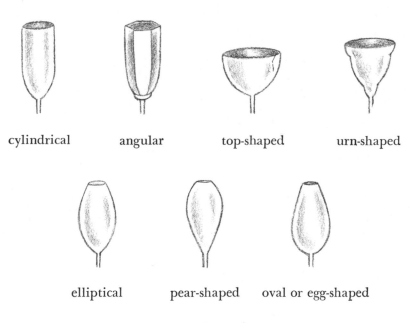

cylindrical   angular   top-shaped   urn-shaped

elliptical   pear-shaped   oval or egg-shaped

Erect Capsules

As it grows, the capsule changes its form and color. A young capsule is nearly always pale green and slender. When dry, it shrinks a good deal. A mature capsule is usually yellowish or reddish-brown and well filled out. It contains spores that are ripe and ready to be scattered. When dry, it retains its shape almost com-

pletely. After the spores have been carried off by the
wind, the capsule is empty but the hollow pod retains
its characteristic shape for some time.

Often you can find both young and old capsules
growing side by side in an expanse of moss plants. Extremely young and extremely old capsules should not

cylindrical,   cylindrical,   globular   pear-shaped with
horizontal   curved   neck distinct

angular,   ovate or   cylindrical,
horizontal   egg-shaped,   hanging down
                   pointed

Capsules not Erect

be used together for study. A very old capsule often
becomes dark, decayed, or broken. The ideal time to
study capsules is in autumn or early winter when the
spores in most capsules mature. Others occasionally
mature in spring and summer.

Capsules come in all shapes—round, angular, pear-shaped, oval, and egg-shaped. Some have the symmetry of miniature urns. When you consider the shape and position of the capsule, do not include the operculum.

Although most mosses reproduce by gametes and spores, some of the less common mosses reproduce by simple cell division. In this vegetative form of reproduction, small budlike bodies—known as *gemmae*—reproduce the plants. Gemmae are minuscule buds composed of a cell or cluster of cells that separate from the parent plant and form new cells. One cell splits into two, two become four, four divide into eight, and so on. Occasionally in this asexual reproduction, tiny parts of the stem, branches, or leaves become detached and grow into new plants.

In any phase of growth, it is fascinating to examine moss plants. Whether the capsule is full blown or budding—even when no fruit is found—the tufts of leaves and carpets of lush green moss hold a world of surprises.

·3·

How They Grow

Mosses are divided into three orders: *Sphagnales* or peat mosses; *Andreaeales,* an order including only one species, Andreaea; and *Bryales* or true mosses. *Bryales* is the large, familiar order containing many families, each of which has many genera (classes) with several species. Although peat moss and Andreaea differ in structure from true mosses, all three orders of mosses have two specific ways of growing—erect or creeping.

Acrocarpous mosses have stems that grow erect. They have barely any branches, or occasionally none at all, and their fruit grows at the tip of the stem. *Pleurocarpous* mosses creep along the ground. Their stems lie prostrate, the fruit usually growing on short side branches. Sometimes they gently ascend and the fruit grows on the sides of the stem. Acrocarpous

21

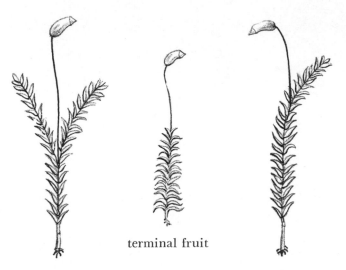

terminal fruit

fruit appearing laterally
by forking of stem

fruit appearing laterally
by new growth of plant

Acrocarpous Mosses

mosses stand straight and full like tiny trees. Pleurocarpous mosses are thin and feathery.

The tiny seta of the capsule on the erect mosses always grows at the tip of the moss stem. If the fruit
appears to be growing from the side of the stem, it is
because new growth has pushed the seta sideways, or
because the stem of the plant forks at the end. When
the seta grows at the tip of the moss stem or branch,
the fruit is called *terminal*. If the seta grows from the
side of the stem, or is on a very short side branch, the
fruit is called *lateral*. All pleurocarpous mosses grow
lateral fruit. The setae of both terminal and lateral
fruit are usually yellow or red.

Moss plants grow by themselves, either in scattered places or crowded together. When acrocarpous plants

stem prostrate
fruit on a short lateral branch

stem ascending
fruit on side of stem

Pleurocarpous Mosses

with erect or ascending stems grow close together, they form deep, mossy mats. If you look closely, the mat is like a dense, miniature forest. When the pleurocarpous plants with their prostrate stems and branches inter-weave, they form thin, flat, tangled carpets. Where certain plants have grown together, you might find clumps of erect green moss in separated tufts that look like plush pincushions.

The main stems of the acrocarpous mosses may not have branches at all or some may branch by forking at the tips. Pleurocarpous mosses, on the other hand, often have numerous lateral branches that grow on opposite sides of the main stem like a feather—*pin-*

nately. Some of these pinnate branches may branch again to grow *bipinnately*. And, some of the bipinnate branches may branch growing *tripinnately*. Some pleurocarpous mosses have main stems that branch out only near the tip of the stem, like the branches of a tree. Other plants do not branch in strictly regular pinnate, bipinnate, tripinnate, or treelike fashion. They branch out irregularly in many ways. On the same primary stem one branch may be pinnate, the next one bipinnate, and others tripinnate, and treelike.

Sometimes the larger primary stem of a pleurocarpous moss is a creeping stem. The smaller secondary stems grow erect or ascending, usually branched. If this is the case, examine the plant carefully. The erect, secondary stems of the pleurocarpous mosses are easy to mistake for the erect stems of an acrocarpous moss.

Individual plants of the acrocarpous, or erect mosses, can be easily detached. Even when different kinds of erect mosses are mixed, it is easy to separate them, particularly if the leaves and capsules of the mosses are dissimilar. For instance, the erect Extinguisher Moss has broad leaves and short setae with long peaked capsules. It is easy to distinguish from the Hairy Cap Moss which has narrow leaves and long setae with hairy, elliptical capsules.

The pleurocarpous mosses are much more tricky to detach than their acrocarpous relatives. Their prostrate stems crawl along the surface weaving such

stems forked

Branching of Acrocarpous Mosses

pinnate   bipinnate   tripinnate   tree-like

irregular   arranged in   primary stem creeping
                   clusters   secondary stems erect
                                        or ascending

Branching of Pleurocarpous Mosses

snarled mats that it can be quite a challenge to separate them. One species of pleurocarpous moss may grow on top of another species and conceal it. At times the creeping stems and branches of the same species of moss may be so firmly interwoven that it is almost impossible to separate them.

Extinguisher Moss   Hairy Cap Moss

Creeping mosses seem deliberately designed to fool you. For example, you might collect an apparently good-fruited specimen of a creeping moss. Then, upon examining it carefully, you may find that the fruit of another moss, hidden underneath, has pushed through the conspicuous growth on the surface. It is easy to mistake this capsule for the fruit that belongs to your specimen.

More sophisticated plants, like flowers and trees, depend upon roots to absorb their food and moisture. Conducting cells carry the food through the stem and distribute it to all parts of the plant. The leaves, as well as other parts of the plant, are covered with a special layer of cells. The outer walls of these cells contain a substance called *cutin,* a coating which is practically waterproof and gasproof. This watertight coating prevents excessive evaporation and also aids in absorption.

Mosses are not dependent upon roots for water absorption. Instead, they have tiny rootlike hairs called *rhizoids* that anchor the plant and absorb moisture.

Rhizoids (greatly enlarged)

Mosses lack veins to conduct water through the stems and leaves; nor do they have a waterproof coating. Moisture passes by means of *osmosis.* Osmosis is the process by which liquids or gases travel through moist cell walls from cells with a high concentration of a substance to cells with a lower concentration. Moss leaves usually have only a single layer of cells. This simple structure causes mosses to dry easily and to absorb water quickly.

Because of their simple structure, when mosses dry, they can often be revived. Can you picture bringing a dead plant back to life? Try it! After you have collected patches of moss, keep a small piece out of water for a few days, weeks, or months. If you place the dry, stiff piece of moss carefully in water for a few minutes, you can watch it come back to life. Watch how quickly and effortlessly the delicate leaves spring back to a fresh condition—a tiny miracle. Compare that piece with the moss that has remained in water, and you won't see any noticeable difference. Scientists have tried this experiment with moss plants that have remained dry for over one hundred years, and the leaves still expanded rapidly. In another experiment, two different kinds of moss were soaked and dried fifty times. There was no injury to the plants other than fading.

·4·

Leaves

Mosses have many more leaves than branches. But because the plants are so tiny, it is easy to mistake branches for leaves. Leaves usually grow all around the stem and branch, occasionally covering them so thoroughly that the outline of the leaf is not visible. When moist, they spread apart and are easier to see. When dry, they twist and curl or fold against the stem, closely overlapping. Branches are usually cylindrical, particularly when the leaves are closely folded around them. The thin, flat leaves of moss plants never have the stalk one finds on other leaves, but grow directly on the branches and stems. Many moss leaves are large enough to be visible to the naked eye. The largest measures fully one-half inch. Others are visible if you hold them up to the light or against something white.

Some moss leaves are too small to see without a lens.

On the same plant, leaves are often different sizes. Those near the base of the stem, as well as the leaves at the tip, are often smaller and not as well developed as those in the middle. Some plants that reproduce asexually by budding do not bear fruit. On these, the leaves usually grow thicker and larger than the leaves of fruited mosses. When a plant has many branches, the leaves on the stem are often larger than those on the branches.

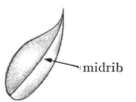

Leaf of the Extinguisher Moss

Catharinaea

A midrib—the central vein in a leaf—also called a *costa*—may or may not be present; also it may be single, double, or forked. The costa on a large leaf like the leaf of an Extinguisher Moss can be seen by holding it up to a window or a lightbulb. It looks like a slender, dark line down the center. Other mosses, such as *Catharinaea,* a common moss that grows extensively on lawns or ravine banks, have midribs that are much wider. Indeed they occupy a large part of the leaf blade.

Leaves of different species vary in shape from hair-like to egg-shaped, but they are never divided into broad sections like the lobes on an oak leaf, nor cut like a maple leaf. On each moss plant there is only one leaf shape.

The leaves of the acrocarpous mosses are either long and narrow or short and broad. Those that are rela-

broader than hair-like   ending in a hair-like tip   ovate or egg-shaped   ovate-oblong   elliptical   nearly round

Acrocarpous Moss Leaves

tively long and narrow may be the same width from the base to the tip like a hair, or broader at the base and gradually narrowed at the tip. Or, the leaf may be the same width throughout ending in a hairlike tip. Short, broad leaves may be egg-shaped, elliptical, or nearly round, or they may be ovate-oblong, shaped like

ovate at base,   ovate at base,
ending in a   ending in
straight tip   a curved tip

Pleurocarpous Moss Leaves

an egg at the base and then longer than wider at the top.

The leaves of pleurocarpous mosses vary less in shape than those of the acrocarpous mosses. They are not easily visible because they are small or closely folded. The most common shape is somewhat oval at the base, ending in a straight or curved tip.

The edge of a moss leaf can be smooth or serrated. On all but a few moss leaves, you will need a magnifying glass to see the sawlike notches on the edge. When they become crinkled, curled, or twisted by drying, leaves are described as *crisped.*

The arrangement and position of leaves are important characteristics in identifying various mosses. Although leaves usually grow around stems and branches, a few mosses like *Fissidens* have leaves arranged in only two rows on opposite sides of the stem. They lie flat like the pinnae of a fern. These leaves are called "erect" when they lie parallel with the stem or "wide-spreading" when they stand out at nearly right angles to the stem. They are called "erect-spreading" or "not wide-spreading" when they are somewhere between erect and wide-spreading. When leaves look as if they are being blown in one direction by the wind, they are referred to as "turned to one side" or *secund*. In some pleurocarpous mosses the leaves are arranged in two rows that curve and turn in opposite directions,

leaves on stem and branches

leaves in two opposite rows (Fissidens)

leaves erect

wide-spreading

turned to one side (secund)

curved and turned in opposite directions

Arrangement of Leaves

giving a braided appearance along the stem and branches.

Often there is a difference between the position of the leaves when they are moist from when they are dry. For instance, leaves that are wide-spreading when moist may become so closely folded when dry that they become erect.

Moss plants are many shades of green. Some are whitish or bluish green, some are golden or yellowish green. Others are bright, olive, or dark green. There is often a variation in color on the same plant because the oldest leaves turn brown or dark, while the youngest are usually pale green.

The predominant color of the plant is determined by the leaves along the central portion of the stem. The characteristic color of moss plants appears when they are healthy and normal, but the color is often affected by the various conditions under which the plant grows. For instance, you might find that the color of moss plants collected and grown indoors is slightly different from the same kind of plant growing outside in a woodlot.

It is always simpler to study and identify fruited mosses. However half of the common species can be identified without the aid of a capsule, if you carefully examine the leaves.

·5·

Mistaken or Misnamed

The name "moss" is commonly applied to a number of plants that are not actually mosses but which closely resemble moss. Some differ in structure, growth, or color. But often, looking like a carpet of moss, the plants cluster and form a solid mat on the ground or on old tree trunks.

Liverworts or hepatics, relatives of the mosses, often confuse people. They are frequently found growing alongside mosses in the shady retreats of the forests or on the damp banks of ravines. These delicate plants have no defense against loss of water due to evaporation. They quickly wither when exposed to dry air or bright sunlight. But, like the mosses, many species revive after long periods when they appeared dead.

Leafy liverworts, sometimes called *scale mosses,* are

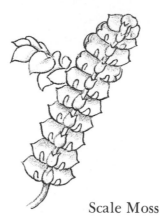

Scale Moss

the species of liverworts most commonly mistaken for moss. Dark green, they have leafy stems that lie flat, gently ascend, or stand erect. The leaves are rounded or, unlike mosses, lobed, or cleft, often curving at the tips. Two rows of leaves grow from the stem, one on each side, with a third row of modified leaves on the underneath part of the stem. Plants are flat, almost papery thin, and have two distinct surfaces. The flattened appearance of the stems and the peculiar shape of the leaves distinguish them from the mosses.

True liverworts have neither a stem, nor leaves. Because of this, they are not as frequently confused with mosses as are leafy liverworts. Finely textured, they look like thin, leathery leaves laid flat. They cling to the earth, rocks, or logs, attached on the undersurface by numerous *rhizoids* that absorb moisture. Liverworts can be long and slender, or lobed, and forked.

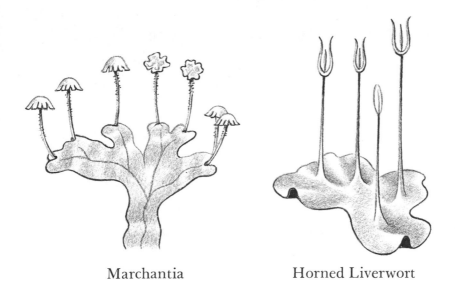

Marchantia   Horned Liverwort

A few grow like tiny flat ribbons about as long as one's little finger. The next time you notice a flat, creeping, rather fleshy looking plant, with rounded lobes on its leaflike body, examine it closely. It may be a liverwort —the simple flowerless plant that was one of the first land plants in the earth's history.

Like mosses, liverworts—the other member of the phylum Bryophyta—also have male and female sex organs. One species of liverwort (*Marchantia*) has a peculiar umbrella-like structure that rises about an inch above the flat plant body. In some of these umbrellas, eggs are carried; in others, sperm are carried. When it rains, the male sperm swim or are splashed from one umbrella structure to another to fertilize the eggs, much in the same manner as the mosses. A liverwort opens its umbrellas, not to avoid the rain

but to catch it. Sometimes the sporophytes of a liverwort are smaller than an eyelash. If you explore moist
places you may even find a Horned liverwort with
sporophytes that look like Pygmy pitchforks.

Perhaps the plants most often mistaken for mosses
are the tiny *lichens*. They are the most primitive and
widespread land plants on earth. There are many vari-
eties but most types fit into one of three groups: crust-
like (crustose), leaflike (foliose), or mossy and shrub-
like (fruiticose).

It is the last of these groups that is so easily confused
with mosses. Fruiticose lichens are often quite beautiful. One striking variety is the British Soldier, or
Lighthouse lichen. Its tiny, green stalks, barely an
inch tall, have bright vermilion tops. The red tips
look like match heads, or miniature lighthouses.
Against the pale green stalks, they are as colorful as
some wildflowers.

The fruiticose lichen most frequently mistaken for
moss is the pearly gray-green shrubby lichen called
Reindeer Moss. It grows from northern New England
north to the arctic tundra. It serves as winter food for
huge herds of caribou, reindeer, and musk ox, as well
as mice and ground squirrels. Even during summer,
when other plants are available, animals nibble on
this delicious lichen. Reindeer Moss is often eaten by
the people of Norway and is said to be crisp and agree-
able. The French, on their travels through the Cana-

dian woods in pursuit of fur trade with the Indians, boiled Reindeer Moss and ate it when their provisions were exhausted.

Although mosses often grow on cliffs near the sea, they never grow in salt water. Some species of algae are mistakenly called "sea mosses." In reality they belong with lichens and fungi—a different plant group from the mosses. They are actually seaweeds.

Irish moss is an algae found in the waters of the western coast of Ireland, England, Europe, and on the eastern coast of the United States. For hundreds of years Irish peasants have used this purplish-brown seaweed as food. In New England, Irish moss is collected by the thousands of tons as a source of vegetable gelatin and used as a thickener in puddings, ice cream, and the like. If you see "carrageen" on a box, you will know it is another name for Irish moss. Ceylon "moss" is another seaweed used in the East for its nutritional value as well as the consistency it adds to other dishes.

On land, there are many other plants falsely referred to as mosses. "Club mosses," sometimes called ground pines, resemble true mosses only in general appearance. They are larger, coarser, more robust plants than true mosses and they belong to the third phylum of plant life. They are actually relatives of the ferns.

These plants are easy to identify. Their name is derived from the curious club-shaped reproductive

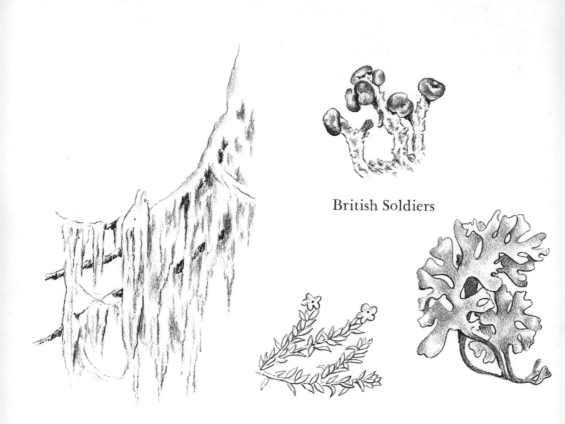

British Soldiers

Spanish Moss   Flowering Moss   Irish Moss (enlarged)

structures they bear at the tops of some of their branches. These branches have stiff evergreen leaves. Fossil ancestors of club mosses have been found dating back to the Carboniferous Age. Their stems were more than ninety feet long.

Modern club mosses are smaller—about ten inches tall. "Stag's horn moss" is a popular name for the species in some localities. The commonest kind of club moss (*Lycopodium*) is used extensively for decora-

Reindeer Moss (enlarged)

Crutose Lichen
(fruiting bodies enlarged)

Club Moss

tions at Christmas time throughout the United States. In some states, there are laws against collecting it because of the danger of extermination.

"Spanish moss," or "Florida moss," hangs conspicuously in long gray tufts from the high branches of trees in the south. The tiny strands of black, hairlike fiber that form the core of this plant are sometimes collected and used instead of horsehair for stuffing furniture. "Spanish moss" is actually a member of the pineapple family. This puts it in the flowering group of plants, along with "Flowering moss" which grows in the pine barrens of New Jersey and southward.

Once you become familiar with mosses—how they live and where they grow—you will find it a simple task to distinguish them from the other plants that are misnamed or commonly mistaken for moss.

· 6 ·

Importance of Mosses

Mosses may seem like rather humble members of the plant kingdom, but they are of great importance. Tens of thousands of years ago these tiny plants played a vital role in making the land fit for habitation. After the primitive plants—the algae and fungi—provided a small amount of soil in which mosses could grow, seeds drifted in, carried by birds and wind. Mosses created a resting place for the seeds of grasses, herbs, shrubs, and familiar trees such as willows, poplars, and birches. Berry bushes grew lavishly, beckoning small wildlife. Then came the jack pines, spruces, and finally the stately white-and-red pines. Gradually, more and larger animals evolved as the plant cover grew and provided the food they needed.

Mosses are still important to soil production. They

grow on bare rocks, in the cracks of cliffs and ledges, and in thin layers of soil. Their rhizoids, or rootlike hairs, push into the small pores in rock. As they grow, they often split tiny particles off the stony surface. Rhizoids secrete substances which gradually convert the rock into new soil. As moss decays, season after season, it forms enough soil to anchor the roots of larger plants. Centuries must pass before a barren rocky surface is transformed into a luxuriant growth of vegetation. Mosses have a great restorative power when catastrophes, such as volcanic eruptions, strip the land bare of life.

Besides producing new soil, moss is important to soil conservation. Covering much of the forest floor with a heavy carpet, the simple structure of moss enables it to absorb rainfall easily. Where extensive growth occurs, water gradually soaks into the earth instead of running off the surface, thus preventing erosion and flooding. Mosses also retain moisture in the ground, keeping it from drying out.

Peat mosses are distinctive and economically important. Peat-forming mosses are called *Sphagnum*. They are found so exclusively in swamps and bogs that they are sometimes known as swamp mosses. Sphagnum is usually erect and varies in color from pale to bright green. This moss rarely bears fruit. The leaves are sharply pointed or spoon-shaped, closely folded, and overlapping or spreading. Their construction is especially adapted to absorb up to twenty-five times their weight in water. They have many branches, arranged in clusters along the stems. These branches, shorter and more crowded at the tips of the stem, form a conspicuous head.

Peat Moss

Each plant grows rapidly at its tip, leaving dead leaves still attached to the stem. The dead parts accumulate to form floating mats. The mats grow larger and larger in size and thickness—from two to four inches a year—as plant debris of previous years decays slowly and occupies the surface. Eventually this accumulation forms peat which is a dark brown or blackish mass of partially decayed vegetation. All sorts of marsh plants from mosses to trees, compose peat.

After a time the growth of Sphagnum mats in a lake may close the water entirely. The resulting mat of soaking wet but apparently solid stuff is called a bog. Finally, what was once a thriving, open lake may become a deep deposit of peat. In this way large Sphagnum mats may increase the available land surface, so that other plants, grasses, shrubs, and trees may grow there. When walking on such a mat, one is sometimes alarmed at the spongy underfooting. What is more surprising is that each step jars all the vegetation. Imagine stepping on a surface and making shrubs and trees move!

Peat moss is important because it can be removed in deep layers, compressed further, dried, and used for fuel. But it is used only in countries like Ireland and in Scandinavia where it is plentiful and coal is scarce, or costly. People cut blocks of peat and pile it in the sun to dry. When it is compressed into compact bricks, it forms a much better fuel than in its natural loose state. Peat burns with a dense black smoke and leaves a great deal of ash. If it were used profusely, it would probably pollute the air in the way that coal does. It has been estimated that there is enough peat in the United States to supply fuel needs for almost a century.

Peat is the first step in making coal. If the peat becomes buried deeply at the bottom of the bog beneath sediments of mud, it becomes greatly compressed. At the same time, it is cut off from contact with the air. Chemical changes take place in the peat, and over a period of millions of years it is transformed from decayed vegetation to coal.

Most peat bogs are the result of the glaciers of ten thousand years ago. Enormous blocks of ice gouged hollows in the earth. When they melted, water filled the holes and they were gradually covered with vegetation. Peat is found chiefly in high latitudes; however, Dismal Swamp, in Virginia, is a fine example of a low-latitude peat bog.

Peat bogs tend to preserve vegetation or animal remains that become buried in them. Sometimes the leaves of plants which compose peat are so well preserved that it is possible for botanists to determine the species to which they belonged. Human and animal bodies have been found well preserved in peat bogs after a lapse of several centuries. Weapons, tools, and armor of the distant past have been buried along with them.

Peat is also valuable to nurserymen because it is so absorbable. It holds water like cotton and is used for packing the roots of plants to prevent them from drying out during shipment. This same absorbable quality makes it useful in a garden as a mulch. It can be worked into the soil or placed on the surface to make the soil loose and to hold water.

The pale, spongelike leaves are filled with hollow

cells that soak liquid with great rapidity. Thus peat makes an ideal surgical dressing with which to pack wounds when prepared cotton wool is not available. Large quantities have been used for this purpose in wars, particularly during World War I.

If you go to a stable, you are apt to see peat spread over the floor as a stable litter. It performs the same duty as kitty litter.

Like almost any vegetable matter, peat has been adapted for making paper, although most paper is now made from wood pulp. In certain localities it is used as a filling for mattresses and pillows. And because it is a nonconducting substance, it is often wrapped around steampipes or packed in the walls of houses as insulation.

In terms of economic value, the Sphagnums are the most important of all the Bryophytes.

·7·

A Mini-World of Mosses

You can have your own mini-world—soil, air, water and mosses—if you collect different kinds of moss and plant them together in a glass globe, glass dish, or apothecary jar, to form a terrarium.

The tools for making a terrarium are right around your house, and the plants may be as near as a neighboring woodlot, or park. When you collect mosses, gather them generously, at least two square inches at a time, to allow for possible damage when separating them. Try to collect enough of the substance on which they grow so that you do not disturb the rhizoids. You will need some coarse gravel or pebbles, a handful of charcoal, and a small amount of soil. If you don't have charcoal, you can buy it at supermarkets, hardware stores, or nurseries. Ground up briquets are fine.

49

When you have everything you need, place a one-inch level of gravel or pebbles in the bottom of the glass container for drainage. Add a thin layer of soil and a handful of crushed charcoal for soil sweetener. Arrange the soil high on one side to "landscape" it. Put the tallest mosses in the background. For character, add a stone or two or a bit of driftwood. Don't pack the soil too tight. Place patches of various mosses over the surface next to each other, not on top of one another. Sprinkle lightly with water and set in a cool place out of the sunlight for a few days. This gives the plants a chance to settle and begin to show signs of growth.

A terrarium is a microworld, self-sufficient enough so that it can live for months within its own climate. The vegetable matter in the soil produces carbon dioxide for the moss to breathe. The plants exhale oxygen which in turn is absorbed by the vegetable matter.

Everything recycles, including water. The moss absorbs moisture from the soil, then sends the vapor back into the air. Next it collects on the glass and runs back into the soil. A little experience will show you how much sun and how much moisture are required. Too much sun will make the plants dry too quickly. Too much moisture, without enough sun, will make the plants mold.

It is interesting to gather moss plants with very young fruit and watch the capsules grow. When you

have collected various mosses, or are examining them outdoors through a magnifying glass, look closely to see if the moss plants are erect and if their capsules are on stalks which terminate the stem. If they grow this way, then they are acrocarpous. If they creep with the capsules growing out laterally from the main stem, they are pleurocarpous.

Hundreds of species of mosses abound in our woods, swamps, and meadows. Although you may not be able to recognize many of the mosses by name, you will find a new pleasure in wandering through the cool forests, the shady ravines, or the sphagnum-filled bogs. Mixed among the luxuriant tangle of plant life are these dwarf members of the land flora who have clung to their moist habitats for millions of years.

Glossary

ACROCARPOUS: Mosses that have their fruit arranged at the tip of an erect stem or on a well-developed branch.

ACROCARPOUS MOSSES:

Acrocarpous

Andreaea: This moss is the only member of the order Andreales. It is one of the few mosses that is dark brown to black in color, especially when dry. Andreaea is a crisped black moss whose brittle leaves are densely matted together. It differs from Bryales, the true mosses, because of the structure of the capsule which is barely noticeable. The fruit is the same dark color as the rest of the plant and the seta is short, rising only slightly above the tip of the stem or branch. Andreaea grows mostly in mountainous regions, on granite or rock, but never on limestone. The "Old Man of the Mountain," in the granite state of New Hampshire, is cloaked by a luxuriant growth of this little moss.

Andreaea

Bryum

Catharinaea

Dicranium

Encalypta

Bryum: This erect moss grows profusely on the rich soil around the roots of trees and in shaded and moist woodlands. Broad-leaved and very green, it is a moss of great beauty. One species has a leafless erect stem with a rosette of leaves at the top. From the center of the rosette the stalk grows with its drooping spore capsule.

Catharinaea: A common moss that grows extensively on lawns or ravine banks.

Dicranium: One of the most beautiful of the woodland acrocarpous mosses is also known as the Crane's Bill Moss. This lustrous yellow-green moss forms thick carpets on soil, stones, and around the base of trees. The beaked capsule on the long stalk is shaped like a heron's bill from which it gets its name.

Encalypta: One of the smaller moss plants, this is known as the Extinguisher Moss. It grows to about an inch in height and prefers the limestone rocks of mountainous regions. Its leaves are rather large and tongue-shaped. The covering of the capsule extends below it, resembling an old-fashioned candle extinguisher.

Fissidens: This moss is found in many locations and contains many species. You will recognize it by its leaves which grow in two flattened rows like the scale mosses or liverworts. It grows to a few inches in height, with tiny paired leaves. You can find it in almost any damp place on the ground—in moist woods, or on wet rocks along streams. Sometimes it comes to life on the shaded earth in greenhouses, but is rarely found at the base of trees or on decaying wood.

Fissidens

Grimmia: This is the only one of the dusky colored mosses that can be found growing on trees. The stems of each plant branch by forking, and they are often ascending instead of erect. In contrast to the smooth capsules of other rock mosses, Grimmia is easily recognized in its reproductive state by the hairy covering on the spore capsules.

Grimmia

Mnium: A moss with delicate glossy leaves, so thin that they are almost transparent. Many species of Mnium are common and easily recognized by their broad flat leaves. This erect moss often forms bright green beds in the swampy ground surrounding woodland springs.

Mnium

Polytrichum: Also called the Hairy Cap Moss, Bird Wheat, or Pigeon Wheat, this coarse, vigorous plant reaches a height of four to six inches. The hairy covering of the spore capsule gives it its name. It is commonly found in pastures, fields, and woodlands. Because it has the ability to drive out grasses, farmers consider it a pest.

Shistostega: A rare moss, found underneath logs and hidden away in crannies at the entrances to caves where the light hits. Shistostega is known as the

Polytrichum

Shistostega

luminous moss because it glows in the dark in a golden-green color similiar to a cat's eyes. The glow seems to come from the ground beneath the little plants because it radiates from the rootlike portions of the moss. These have cells which refract any light entering the cave or dark hole.

Sphagnum: Peat-forming mosses found almost exclusively in swamps and bogs.

Sphagnum

ANTHERIDIA: Male sex organs containing sperms called Antheridium.

ARCHEGONIA: Female sex organs, each containing a female egg called Archegonia.

BIPINNATE: Twice pinnate, its pinnate branches branch again.

Bract

BRACT: A leaflike part, usually situated at the base of a flower.

BRYALES: True mosses.

BRYOPHYTA: The phylum of plants that includes mosses and liverworts.

Calyptra

CALYPTRA: The thin hood covering the operculum or lid of the capsule.

CAPSULE: Often spoken of as the fruit; the small pod containing the spores.

CARRAGEEN: Irish moss.

Capsule

CILIA: Hairlike projections whose movements cause the cell to move through surrounding liquid.

COSTA: Midrib of a moss leaf.

CRISPED: Curled up, twisted, or wrinkled.

CUTIN: The substance covering the outer walls of plant cells, both waterproof and gasproof.

ERECT: Upright. Leaves are described as erect when they are nearly parallel to the stem.

Erect

FORKED: Divided at the tip.

FRUIT: Same as a capsule; the sack containing the spores.

FRUITED: Bearing fruit.

FRUIT-STALK: The seta or stem of the fruit.

GAMETES: The sex cells which may unite to form a new individual cell.

Gametophyte

GAMETOPHYTE: The sexual stage in the alternating generations of plants.

GEMMAE: Small budlike bodies capable of reproducing the plant.

Gemmae

HABITAT: The natural locality of a plant or animal.

HAIRLIKE: Without perceptible width.

HEPATICAE: Liverworts, subclass of Bryophyta.

IRREGULARLY BRANCHED: Not regularly pinnate, bipinnate, tripinnate, or treelike.

Irregularly branched

LATERAL: Coming from the side.

LICHEN: A plant which is composed of fungi and algae living together in partnership.

LIVERWORT: Hepaticae, subclass of Bryophyta. Plant relative to moss, often mistaken for it.

Liverwort

LOBED: Divided into broad parts.

MATURE: Ripe. A plant, capsule, or fruit is de-

Operculum

scribed as mature when the spores are ready to be scattered to develop new plants.

MUSCI: Mosses, subclass of Bryophyta.

OPERCULUM: The lid or cap of the capsule that covers the peristome.

OSMOSIS: The passing of liquids or gasses through moist cell walls or other membranes from places with a higher concentration of a substance to those of a lower concentration.

Peristome

PEAT: A piece of partly decayed vegetation from ancient swamps.

PERISTOME: The fringe surrounding the mouth of the capsule beneath the operculum.

PHOTOSYNTHESIS: The process by which chlorophyll, using the sun's energy, manufactures carbohydrates from carbon dioxide and water and releases oxygen.

Pinnate

PHYLA: Plural of phylum. A main division of the plant or animal kingdom.

PINNATE: With branches on either side of the stem in opposite rows.

PLEUROCARPOUS: Mosses that have their fruit arranged laterally on the stem in opposite rows.

Pleurocarpous

PLEUROCARPOUS MOSSES:

The creeping mosses include many of the most showy of the woodland variety. Because of their prostrate way of growing, they frequently cover entire logs and ravine banks. The Fern moss, Plume moss, Tree moss; and Water moss are examples.

Climacium: This tree moss is a larger and more robust plant than most mosses. It is often confused with the Running pine, *Lycopodium*, which is one of the club mosses. The erect treelike shoots of Climacium form dark-green clumps that rise like a tiny forest on the damp earth in woods and swamps. These are the giants of the Bryophytic world, yet they attain a stature of only six inches.

Climacium

Fontinalis: This is one of the creeping mosses which lives entirely submerged in water throughout its life. Its Latin name means "belonging to water." You can find it in streams and ponds but never in stagnant water. Scalelike, brownish-green leaves cover the long slender branches, although sometimes the leaves are golden-green or copper-colored. It is easily recognizable because the large, deeply concave leaves are arranged in three rows, creating a three-sided appearance to the long floating stems with their erect or slightly spreading leaves. Other long-stemmed mosses commonly found in water have finer leaves, wide-spreading, or more or less curved.

Fresh water algae, often found in the same streams with Fontinalis, are long and threadlike.

Fontinalis

Hypnum

Thuidium

This somewhat slimy alga may be distinguished from moss because it does not have leaves.

Hypnum: This is the Plume moss, also known as the Feather moss. Its flattened branches spray out like a miniature evergreen tree. It covers logs and stumps in the cool woods with blankets of deep green.

Thuidium: The scientific name of this moss means "small, feathery branched tree" because of the delicate branching of the plants. The branches subdivide into smaller branches, with leaves so tiny that they are barely visible.

PROTONEMA: The first growth that is produced from the spore. A felted mass of green threads.

REGULARLY BRANCHED: With branches on both sides of the stem, often evenly arranged.

RHIZOIDS: Rootlike hairs attached to the underside of mosses, liverworts, and lichens.

SCALE MOSSES: Leafy liverworts.

SECUND: Turned to one side.

SETA: The stem or stalk of a capsule.

SPERM: One of the male reproductive cells of plants and animals.

SPORE: A minute, dustlike body produced in the fruit of the lower plants that takes the place of seeds in higher plants.

SPOROPHYTE: Capsule and stem of mosses and liverworts.

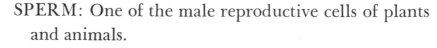

Sporophyte

SPREADING: In reference to the fruit or capsule, coming at the end of the stem or branch.

TERMINAL: Growing at the tip of a moss stem or branch.

TRIPINNATE: Three times pinnate; when the bi-pinnate branches again.

Tripinnate

VEGETATIVE: Growing in some way other than from the spore.

ZYGOTE: The cell or fertilized egg that results from the joining of the pre-existing male sperm and female egg.

Zygote

Bibliography

Dunham, Elizabeth Marie. *How to Know the Mosses.* Boston: The Mosher Press, 1951

Gruenberg, Benjamin C. *Biology and Man.* Boston: Ginn & Co., 1944.

Hedrick, U. P. *Sturtevant's Edible Plants of the World.* New York: Dover Publications, 1972.

Hylander, Clarence J. *The World of Plant Life.* New York: Macmillan Co., 1960.

Moon, T. J. et al. *Modern Biology.* New York: Henry Holt, 1951.

Robbins, W. W. et al. *Botany: An Introduction to Plant Science.* New York, London, Sydney: John Wiley & Sons, 1967.

Wildwell, Otto W.; Sherman, Nina Henry; Curtis, Francis D., *Everyday Biology.* New York, Boston, Chicago, London, Atlanta, Dallas, Columbus, San Francisco: Ginn & Co., 1941

Index

acrocarpous mosses, 21-24, 31-32, 52
algae, 9-10, 39, 43
alternation of generations, 12
Andreaeales, 21
antheridia, 12
antheridium, 12
archegonia, 12-13
archegonium, 12-13

bogs, 44, 46-47, 52
branches, moss, 23-24, 29, 45
British Soldier (Lighthouse) lichen, 38
Bryales, 21
Bryophyta, 9-10, 37, 48

calyptra, 16-17
capsules, 13, 16-20, 22, 24, 34
carrageen, 39
Catharinaea, 31

cell division, 20
Ceylon "moss," 39
chlorophyll, 10, 13
cilia, 12
"club mosses," 39-41
coal, 46-47
conservation, soil, 44
costa (midrib), 30-31
cutin, 27

eggs, 12-13, 37
Extinguisher Moss, 24, 30-31

ferns, 9-10
Fissidens, 32-33
"Florida moss," 41-42
"Flowering moss," 42
fruit, 8, 13, 16, 21, 22, 26-27, 30, 44
  lateral, 22
  terminal, 22

63